Why Join a Small Church?

Why Join a Small Church?

John Benton

CHRISTIAN
FOCUS

Copyright © John Benton 2008

ISBN 978-1-84550-407-6

Published in 2008
by
Christian Focus Publications,
Geanies House, Fearn, Ross-shire,
IV20 1TW, Scotland, UK

www.christianfocus.com

Cover design by Daniel van Straaten

Printed and bound by CPD, Wales

Contents

INTRODUCTION

HOW COULD WE DRIVE PAST?.. 7

CHAPTER 1

REASONS TO TAKE UP THE CHALLENGE.. 9

CHAPTER 2

PROBLEMS YOU MAY FACE 17

CHAPTER 3

WHY IT IS A TRAGEDY IF SMALL CHURCHES CLOSE............................. 25

CHAPTER 4

HOW TO MAKE A SMALL CHURCH A GREAT CHURCH............................ 37

CHAPTER 5

ENCOURAGEMENT FOR THE TASK.. 47

EPILOGUE

AN IRRECOVERABLE MOMENT? 57

INTRODUCTION
HOW COULD WE DRIVE PAST?

A Christian married couple I know of had to move out of London and leave their church to go north with the husband's job.

Much to the surprise of some of their long-term Christian pals they began attending the little and very local Anglican church in the village to which they had moved. The Christian friends of the couple had concerns. The church was small, the teaching was not heretical but it was not great, and there was nothing there for their four children. It was while talking through these concerns one evening with one of their friends that the husband made a comment which was highly significant. He said, 'How could we drive past one church to go to another?' They felt, before God, they just could not do it.

They refused to dismiss the little church because it was in a poorly state. They were more concerned to help Christ's cause there than they were for their own immediate welfare or 'enjoyment' of the ministry.

Over time, they approached the vicar and with his blessing began to run a Sunday school in parallel with the morning service for their children and the children of one other family. From there things began to take off. The church grew a little and when they had to move away three years later they left behind Christian friends who had been really encouraged by their involvement.

There was a real cost to them taking this difficult option to join a small fellowship. But certainly a blessing resulted for that local church. Whilst not a comfortable or 'prudent' thing to do, getting involved in a struggling church may be, in God's goodness, a mission from the Lord. It can be really significant in shaping that church's future and encouraging others to join. Just a few folk, a few young single people or just one or two families, can make all the difference.

To join a big and thriving church is not always wrong, but it is frequently the easy option. To join a little needy congregation is not a decision to be taken lightly. It will probably require far more guts, love, resilience and spiritual exertion. But how the devil would love to herd Christians into a few big city centre churches, getting them to travel miles from their communities, and leaving vast tracts of our country with no viable witness for the gospel.

This booklet is written as a plea for Christians to think again about getting involved with a small church. Ask yourself the question, 'How can we drive past one church to go to another?'

CHAPTER 1
REASONS TO TAKE UP THE CHALLENGE

God loves to do things which the world has written off as impossible. That is his trademark, Luke 1:37. In particular when God does something wonderful he likes to start with something so small; something that people don't even notice. In encouraging you to join a small church I am inviting you to get on board God's agenda.

- Think about it. If you were going to create a universe what would you begin with? God created it all out of nothing, Romans 4:17. And you can't get smaller than nothing.

- Think about it. If you were going to make a way to save the world of nature from coming catastrophe, where would you start? Faced with that problem, God looked to a small church. It was made up of one man named Noah and his family. Just eight people. Under God's direction they built the ark and the rest is history.

- Think about it again. If you were going to save the world, where would you begin? As he thought about the need for a nation and then a worldwide family through which he could bring his salvation plan to fruition, God started with two old people. In fact they were two old people in whom life had very much begun to wane. They were unable to have children. Their names were Abram and Sara. But to those two God promised descendants more numerous than the sand on the seashore and blessing for the whole world. God started with what was small, old and in some senses dead. Small, old and dead. Those are three adjectives which have been used to describe many little churches.

- Think about it a fourth time. If you were going to save that nation from slavery and oppression under the greatest super-power of the day, where would you commence? God called one 80 year old shepherd to do the job. It was God's hand upon Moses which brought Israel out of slavery in Egypt.

- Think about it once more. If you were going to save mankind from sin and eternal destruction and open for them the gates of heaven, where would you start? God sent one man. Actually to begin with he was a tiny baby. His name was Jesus.

'How can you get something from nothing? It's impossible!'

'How can just eight people be right and all the rest of the world be wrong? It's impossible!'

'How can two barren senior citizens change the course of history? It's impossible!'

'How can an old shepherd overturn a totalitarian super-power?' It's impossible!'

'How can a baby in a manger be the Saviour of mankind? It's impossible!'

Absolutely right. That's why God did these things.

It is a risk to get involved with a small church. It takes faith in the living God. There are few people and few resources. In fact there can be next to nothing – except God. Jesus promised, 'Where two or three come together in my name, there am I with them.' And his parting promise to his disciples did not depend on large numbers either, 'Surely, I am with you always, to the very end of the age.'

It seems as if you would be taking a big gamble to join a small church. But God loves what is small, and if he decides to work by his mighty power you will witness a miracle. It will not be explicable in terms of human resources, what can be done through the power of wealth or numbers of people. You will be involved from the beginning in a work of God and have a real story to tell your grandchildren! 'Let me tell you what the LORD did. I was there...'

So, Christian, let me set out seven reasons for you to throw in your lot with a little church.

1. The big churches can spare you

We thank God for the big churches of our nation. There are great ministries of great Bible expositors who are so helpful to so many and hence a large congregation comes together. But those same great preachers would agree that the last thing in the world they are seeking to do is to build their own empires or make their hearers spiritually dependent on them. No, rather they seek to build people to maturity in Christ so that they can have ministries of their own. This is the work of a pastor/teacher, 'to prepare God's people for works of service,' Ephesians 4:11, 12. Many large churches run excellent training courses or apprentice schemes. But even apart from those, if you are under good ministry you are being prepared for works of service. And in these days there are many works of service to be done in small churches. The numbers of people going along to the big church are so great that they can spare you.

2. The small churches need you

The big churches don't really need you. There are plenty of others. But the little churches do need you. Many small fellowships are on the brink of closure. The people there need reinforcing. They need encouragement. They need the breath of fresh air which perhaps you can bring. And there is such a thing as 'critical mass'. From nuclear physics we learn that as you build up the amount of radioactive uranium at a certain point a chain reaction kicks off. It can be like that with a small church. Just two or three extra servant-hearted Christians and things start to happen. Things begin to turn around and instead of facing closure the church can be looking at an open door into the future.

3. *Small churches give opportunities to serve*

If you attend a large church which runs like a well-oiled machine often all the key jobs in the church are filled. Indeed those key posts may not even be open to ordinary Christians. Paid staff, with counselling diplomas and formal theological training, is the order of the day. Without perhaps intending to, the big church frequently invites you to simply be a passenger. Turn up on Sunday and do your homework for the fellowship group and pray, but that is about it. Meanwhile you may have a gift which is never really used. You might be someone who is able to listen and sympathetically advise folk going through troubles. But you would not be given much of an opportunity in the big church. You might have a reasonable gift of preaching or a fairly passable talent for music. However, you would not get a look in at the big church. But you would be a true God-send to a smaller congregation. So think about joining a small church. Don't let the big church bury your talent, Matthew 25:18. Don't become deskilled through lack of opportunity.

4. *Small churches enjoy closer fellowship*

Even the larger congregations recognise the value of small groups. That is why we find cell groups, prayer groups and area fellowship groups and support groups, etc. as part of the timetable for many big churches. Close fellowship with people who we know very well is of enormous value. Here we can share our hearts, our joys and our troubles, without the whole world knowing the intimate details of our lives. Here we find friends who understand us, who will keep confidences and will pray for us. It is just not possible for everyone in a large church to have that depth of intimacy with one another. But it is in a little church. And because of that closeness there is often a richness of shared life which is very special in a congregation with lesser numbers. Sometimes quality does win out over quantity.

5. Smaller churches will stretch you more as a Christian

If you are the athletic kind or the adventurous kind you will enjoy a challenge. Great athletes only develop as they are prepared to push themselves; to take on more and more difficult tests; to run faster, to last longer, to go further. Spiritual development is similar. That is why the writer to the Hebrews uses that great athletic picture of the Christian life as a marathon race, Hebrews 12v1. Being part of a small fellowship brings a greater challenge to our Christianity. It is easy to feel encouraged when you are standing in a vast congregation. It is more difficult to have faith that God can work when you look around and there are so few of you. Our love is tested too. It is easy in a big church for problems between Christians to fester and never be resolved. People simply avoid speaking to each other, making sure their paths never really cross amid the Sunday crowds. In a small church you can't avoid each other. You have to sort things out. So it is that your Christian graces will be stretched. I am not surprised that some of the best Christians I know are from small churches.

6. Small churches offer you a life's work of real significance

Many people live and die but they never achieve anything of lasting significance in life. At the end of their lives they are gone but in one sense it is as if they were never here. As Christians we should have a deep desire to achieve something for God; something of eternal value. All our success in secular employment, the money we have made and the deals we have pulled off, will mean little in the light of eternity. But the work of the local church registers in the realms of 'forever'. People get saved. The Lord gets glorified. Now obviously this is true of every church large or small. But if you are part of a small church your contribution means more. It may well be, without your contribution the church would have folded. 'What have I done with my life?' Perhaps you will be able to answer humbly but honestly, 'I have, under God, been instrumental in keeping the light of Christ shining in an area where otherwise it would have gone out.' That is no mean achievement.

7. Small churches offer you the chance to confound the world
Thank God that in many places in the world today the church is growing astonishingly. One statistic from *The Bible Society* recently was that they estimate that 15,000 people a day in China are turning to Christ. I have a friend working in South America who says it is commonplace where he lives to see people reading their Bibles on the bus as they go to work; so many people are becoming Christians. That is great. But at present it is not like that here. In fact, the world believes that the church of Christ is about to die in the West. They label our society 'post-Christian.' And every time a little church closes they are confirmed in their belief that Christ can be dismissed. O how good it would be for no more churches to close, but instead for them to start growing. How it would get

non-Christians scratching their heads and perhaps to thinking again about Jesus. So join a small church.

What kind of criteria do you use to decide which church to get involved with? Many Christians sadly are guided by some pretty threadbare, not to say worldly benchmarks.

Here are a few I have run into. 'What is the music group like?' 'Is the church building impressive and smart?' 'Are there lots of *fit* girls or *hot* young men in the congregation who perhaps might make me a partner in life?' 'Do the services use the latest technology?' 'Does the pastor wear sharp clothes and have a winning smile?' 'Is the minister famous?' 'What is the coffee like?' 'Are there so many people that I am unlikely to be asked to do anything too onerous and can just relax in the church?' These are factors at which the apostles would be completely astonished. Yet sadly these things do rule the choices of many Christians.

Hopefully our criteria when considering churches are of a rather higher standard than that. 'Is the love of Christ shown in the friendliness of the people?' 'Is the teaching Biblical?' 'Is the church seeking to reach out with the gospel?' Those are much better standards by which to judge a church. But let's be honest, many small churches do meet those criteria. So why not join?

CHAPTER 2
PROBLEMS YOU MAY FACE

Estate agents, in their endeavour to sell properties, have earned a reputation for writing some rather deceptive descriptions of the houses and flats on their books.

A small, poky little dwelling may be described as 'compact.' A house that is very run down and in need of major repair work can be marketed as 'with potential for development.' Something of an old shack which is downright odd and has an unfortunate odour is sometimes advertised as 'having character.' So 'a compact residence of character close to the shops with potential and cosmopolitan views' may well be a tiny dingy flat with a leaky roof and damp walls above the chemist shop in a noisy city High St. They are selling you a load of trouble.

I need to be upfront and honest about trying to get you to think about joining a small church. There can often be problems. I do not want to fall foul of the Trades Descriptions Act! There is a desperate need for Christians to join small churches. But you need to be clear about what you might be taking on.

Therefore I need to list some of the problems you may face if you seek to help a small church.

1. Bad facilities

Small churches rarely have much money. There are only a few to support the work financially. This often means, especially if they are doing their best to maintain a full-time pastor for the little flock, that there is not much cash to spare on repairing the church building. We live at a time when generally speaking the standard of living has increased quite markedly. People have become used to facilities which are well-maintained, clean and smart. Very often it is not like that in a small church. Further, there will not be many good or up-to-date resources for coffee mornings etc. Those who are brave enough to join a small church may not be ashamed of the gospel, but might well find themselves ashamed of the premises. You might well feel that if you invite non-Christian friends along they will be put off by the state of the building before they ever hear the gospel. What can be done about that?

2. Nothing for the children

I was talking to a pastor recently who commented that if all the people over 50 years old were taken away from the churches in his area most of them would cease to exist. Often the congregations of small churches are made up of people who are all 'getting on' in years. If you are a young family with little children, you may well be forced to hesitate before joining a small church. 'There's nothing for my children here,' you realise. What effect is that going to have on them in the long term? Of course, it may well be that if the little church has a warmth about it then your children will be taken to the hearts of the congregation and accommodation somehow made for giving the children a helpful and happy time at church. In such a case the greater danger might be that your children will be spoiled by soft-hearted older saints who are so pleased to see youngsters among them! However, it is not always like that. How can you get involved with a church which is not, at least initially, child-friendly?

3. Discouragement

It is tough for all Christians at the present time in the Western world, whatever the size of our congregation. Aggressive secularism rules the roost and even though under this regime society is disintegrating with the break-down of family life and the increase in violence and all kinds of anti-social behaviour, nevertheless the majority of people think Christianity is totally implausible and not worth giving a second thought. To be a Christian is to be thought a fool. It is to swim against the tide in society.

But clearly people in a little fellowship feel this tide most keenly. They feel discouraged. In reaction they may well adopt a siege mentality. Small churches become very defensive. They feel victimised and rather helpless. They can be over-sensitive to any perceived criticisms. Their agenda is about surviving rather than reaching out with the love of God to a lost world. How do you encourage them to snap out of that and take some risks for God?

4. Resentment and suspicion

The siege mentality I have described can lead to resentment and suspicion of anyone who joins the church and tries to change anything. By implying that change might improve things for the church we can be taken as condemning what has gone on in the past. Over-sensitive about their inadequacies, even Christians may react negatively. Pride often enters the equation too. Sometimes they would rather see the church die and to identify themselves as 'the faithful few' who stayed true to the end, than be prepared to listen to people who have only recently started coming to the church. How do you get around that? It is often a matter of winning hearts and fostering trust. Real fellowship has to be built before a church can move forward. This is not always possible. Even where it is possible it may take a long time.

5. Lack of spiritual life

Obviously there are some churches have completely turned away from the gospel and godly living and promote heresy. I could not encourage you to get involved with them.

But this is certainly not true in many small churches. Often little fellowships are full of faith, hope and love and can be a positive tonic to be involved with. However, I want to paint a worst case scenario so that no one goes into this work of helping small churches blindfold. So we must face the fact that there are other little congregations where the spiritual flames are burning low, with say just a few embers left smouldering. Perhaps the people taking comfort from the thoughts of better times for the church in past years have begun to live in the past and find more security in their traditions than in Christ himself. The sermons have become little more than a repetition of various evangelical clichés and seem detached from real life. Formalism has begun to have its deadening influence. This is a problem which is not easy to deal with. Spiritual deadness may even begin to take its toll on your own spiritual life if you are not careful. Are you strong enough, with God's enabling, to bear the load and to wrestle prayerfully until the Lord revives his people?

(NB. In this situation perhaps listening to the ministry of good Bible expositors from MP3s or internet downloads might be a way of keeping spiritually fed and strong.)

6. Idiosyncrasies

By very nature of what the church is, every church attracts vulnerable and needy people. In many ways it is the glory of the church that we do. The love of God is there. People who are disabled or lonely or unlovely often gravitate to the church. In many large and successful congregations such people (to the church's shame) get ignored. The church doesn't need them. They have got plenty of others coming along. But smaller churches tend to have more time for these folk with their idiosyncrasies. That being so, smaller churches may well attract more than their fair share of such people. This can give a strange 'air' to the church to any new visitor. We can easily be put off by such an atmosphere. It is not 'cool.' It is not 'slick and presentable' by today's standards. Are we going to walk away from such congregations? Are we going to shake off the dust from our feet against them because they are not young, healthy, 'sharp' and attractive in worldly terms?

7. Unimpressive worship

There is a great encouragement from singing great hymns in a big congregation. The emotion of it all can make the hairs on the back of our necks stand up and thrill us deeply. Modern worship with its contemporary music styles and catchy beats lifts many people's spirits and leaves us with a song full of helpful truth which we remember for the rest of the week. Big congregations tend to have a surfeit of people, young and old, with musical gifts for many instruments. But it is seldom like that in a little church. Hymn singing is not the essence of worship. But when there is just a broken down organ or a rather out of tune piano to accompany a few voices trying their best, it hardly feels as if we are making the praise of God glorious. This too can be hard.

So here are some of the problems which we might well meet if we are contemplating taking on the challenge of getting involved with a small church. Seeing such problems might be enough to put us off. But nevertheless, these churches belong to the Lord Jesus Christ. The reputation of the Lord is at stake over the future of every one. Every time a little church closes it gives the watching world one more reason to think that Christ is non-existent, powerless and can be ignored. What reason can I give you, despite the problems, to go and get stuck in? Ultimately none; except, if we love Christ, it has to be done.

Seeing the kinds of difficulties I have outlined here many would counsel that it is easier to plant new churches than try to restore old failing ones. Sometimes that may be true. You can start with a clean sheet of paper and decide the best way forward without having to deal first with difficult old members and out of date traditions. But still there are reasons to believe that helping existing small churches is better.

- *Witness* To start another church where there already is one is to undermine the unity of the church in the eyes of the watching world. 'Why should we believe what you are preaching? You Christians can't even agree yourselves or worship together,' they say.

- *Finance* When a small church closes often its building is sold off. Even apart from the shame of it now becoming a carpet warehouse or a temple of another religion, what happens to the money from the sale? Frequently it gets lost in the central coffers of a failing denomination (never to be seen again?), while the new church plant is either spending money every month on renting a school or trying to get many thousands of pounds together to buy a venue. What a waste of resources.

- *Message* When we church plant while ignoring an existing small church the message being given is not that Christ is the answer, but that our particular brand of church is the answer. This smacks more of our own empire building than building God's kingdom.

- *Discouragement* When a new group of Christians moves in with no respect or hand of friendship for an existing church the obvious implication is that the existing church is not worth bothering with. Yet the Lord calls us to 'encourage one another' (Heb. 10:25).

- *Sheep-stealing* Though church plants are meant to grow by conversions, often they don't. Frequently they grow by taking Christians from other gospel churches in the area.

Obviously there are situations which genuinely require planting new churches. But where there are small struggling churches already in existence, it is far better, whatever the difficulties, if we can help to build up what is already in existence.

CHAPTER 3
WHY IT IS A TRAGEDY IF
SMALL CHURCHES CLOSE

Behind encouraging you to think about getting involved in a small church is the conviction that every community in our land needs a good church. In many places those churches are struggling to survive. But the town or village where they are located desperately needs them.

The reason it is a tragedy when churches close is, of course, because everyone needs to hear the gospel of Jesus Christ and if possible to see it lived out in practical life. When a Bible church closes it usually leaves an area where people have been robbed of the possibility of hearing the gospel. But, in fact, everyone needs to become a Christian and local churches are the God-ordained means of holding out the word of life to the community. So, in order not to forget the main goal in view in supporting small churches let's just remind ourselves, through a brief piece of exposition, of the great and necessary benefits of people becoming Christians.

³Praise be to the God and Father of our Lord Jesus Christ! In his great mercy he has given us new birth into a living hope through the resurrection of Jesus Christ from the dead, ⁴and into an inheritance that can never perish, spoil or fade—kept in heaven for you, ⁵who through faith are shielded by God's power until the coming of the salvation that is ready to be revealed in the last time. ⁶In this you greatly rejoice, though now for a little while you may have had to suffer grief in all kinds of trials. ⁷These have come so that your faith—of greater worth than gold, which perishes even though refined by fire—may be proved genuine and may result in praise, glory and honour when Jesus Christ is revealed. ⁸Though you have not seen him, you love him; and even though you do not see him now, you believe in him and are filled with an inexpressible and glorious joy, ⁹for you are receiving the goal of your faith, the salvation of your souls.

¹⁰Concerning this salvation, the prophets, who spoke of the grace that was to come to you, searched intently and with the greatest care, ¹¹trying to find out the time and circumstances to which the Spirit of Christ in them was pointing when he predicted the sufferings of Christ and the glories that would follow. ¹²It was revealed to them that they were not serving themselves but you, when they spoke of the things that have now been told you by those who have preached the gospel to you by the Holy Spirit sent from heaven. Even angels long to look into these things.

1 Peter 1:3-12

'Why is it worthwhile to be a Christian?' That is the question which is being dealt by the apostle Peter in the New Testament passage quoted above.

People today ask the question because we live in a society shot through with apathy, that doesn't see the point of taking anything seriously. But it was a particularly crucial question for Peter because he writes at a time when Christians were facing suffering for their faith. If church traditions are correct, Peter was writing from Rome where he would soon be martyred himself (crucified upside down) at the command of the emperor Nero. Sadly, even today, especially in Muslim lands, Christians still face persecution and even death for their faith. 'Well, if Christianity might cost you your life, what's the point? Why is it worthwhile to be a Christian?' Here, Peter gives three answers to that question, which will remind us why every person needs to hear the gospel and why therefore every community needs a gospel preaching church.

Because everybody needs a future salvation (vv. 3-5).
Look at verses 3-5. Peter's first answer is that it is worthwhile to be a Christian because of the Christian's future prospects.

Let's be honest, many people today are depressed about life, and mostly the TV or radio news is pessimistic about the future. That's why a lot of people don't bother with it. And if you think of the great writers who have imagined the future they don't paint a very optimistic picture either. I remember at school we had to read H. G. Wells' novel *The Time Machine* in which he imagines travelling 800,000 years forward in time. And what is the situation? Mankind has divided into two species: the Eloi who live in the daylight; and the nocturnal, subterranean Morlocks. The Eloi are soft, weak, rich creatures. The Morlocks are the lower class workers, toiling in their underground factories making everything the Elois need. But like human rats, the Morlocks emerge after dark to prey upon the Eloi and eat them for meat. Wells' nightmare vision of the future showed what he thought would be the end point of the division between the rich and the poor in the world. And the future is equally bleak in Huxley's *Brave New World* or George Orwell's *1984* or in more up-to-date forebodings concerning global warming and an ecological catastrophe.

But over against all this, Peter describes Christians (v. 3) as being in possession of a 'living hope through the resurrection of Jesus Christ from the dead.' That hope, that future prospect is nothing less than a new world, a joyful and eternal 'inheritance' (v. 4). This world is not destined for the dustbin. God will renew it when Jesus comes again, and all that is good and wholesome and lovely will be part of that world to come. Peter stresses three things about this new world, this 'living hope'.

- *Its inception*

  It comes about because of 'the resurrection of Jesus Christ' (v. 3). Peter is conflating two things here. Firstly, this present world is in decline because it is under the curse of God because of human sin. But Jesus paid for our sin when he died on the cross and his resurrection shows that the curse is dealt with. For all who believe there is now eternal life not death. Second, how do we know this coming new, eternal world is real and not just some foolish pipe-dream? We know because Jesus is risen from the dead as the first example of life in the new world.

• *Its occupants*

People have a place in God's new world through 'new birth' (v. 3). Just as this world will be reborn, so the occupants of the world to come are people who have been spiritually reborn. Not to be reborn of God's Spirit is to have no place in God's new world, but to face the fearful prospect of being cast into outer darkness. That is why it is absolutely necessary that people hear the gospel and turn to Christ. But when we become a Christian through personal faith in Christ, God's Holy Spirit comes into our lives and gives us a new heart, making us new inwardly. Whereas we used to resent God, now we love him. Whereas we used to be afraid of God, now we know we are forgiven. You can often see the change in people just by looking at them. Such people are being given a new future and are being prepared for life in God's new world.

• *Its certainty*

Look at verses 4 and 5. Verse 4 tells Christians this inheritance is kept for us and verse 5 tells us that through faith we are kept for it. We can't be lost and it can't be lost – so it's a certainty for all who believe.

Now when this is explained many people are sceptical. They say something like, 'Christianity has blown its credibility by promising too much. I could believe perhaps in some merely spiritual existence after death. But a new world of bodily resurrection and eternal life is too much to swallow!' We can understand people saying that. But the New Testament's answer is that God does not tailor his promises to suit our natural cynicism and sinful unbelief. If he did, he could offer us very little. Rather, God is a big God (he made the universe) and he makes big and wonderful promises. Instead of rejection and judgement there is this certain living hope for all who turn to Christ.

That is the first reason it is worthwhile for people to become Christians. All churches, big or small, which preach the good news of Jesus Christ offer the greatest possible long-term benefit to the people of their communities.

But there is a second reason why everybody needs to hear the gospel.

Because everybody needs a handle on present experience (vv. 6-9).
'All this talk about a new world in the future is all very well, but I need to know how Christian faith can help me now, in this world.' That is what some people say as churches seek to reach out to them for Christ. It is a fair question and Peter turns his attention to the Christian's present experience in these next verses. He tells us two things.

- *First, Christian faith gives us a handle on suffering*
  Look at verses 6 and 7. You see the secular way of life is fine for this world so long as everything is OK.

  But for most people, most of the time, it isn't OK. We get ill, we get made redundant, our relationships break up, we find our work boring, our holiday plans get messed up, the person we love most in the world dies! How do we handle this? After all, if this life is all there is, and it is full of trouble, no wonder lots of people are unhappy.

But you see from verses 6 and 7 the Christian has a completely different handle on trouble. First, we do not see what happens in our lives as random. All our troubles big or small are in God's hands. Second, he allows trouble into our lives to refine our faith and grow us as people. He is like an old fashioned purifier of metals (v. 7) who puts the metal into the fire to melt it, so all the rubbish comes to the surface and can be scooped off, and the genuine gold can remain. So the Christian, who trusts in God, can have a really positive outlook even on trouble. There are so many sad people in our communities who need to be rescued from sad lives by positive Christian faith.

• *Second, Christian faith gives us a source of joy*

It is often interesting to see some of the newspaper headlines on New Year's Eve. One recently talked about the numbers of people likely to be admitted to hospital because of binge drinking that night. Another spoke of the fact that there are usually record numbers of abortions after New Year's Eve, through thoughtless casual sex. Why do people wreck their bodies with alcohol and all the rest? It all speaks of a generation which knows very little real happiness and people who desperate to do something, anything to, feel good, no matter what the consequences.

But, by contrast with that, Christians have a wonderful source of real joy through knowing Jesus Christ. Look at verses 8 and 9. The Christian loves Jesus Christ, first of all for who he is, but also because of how much he has loved us. The Christian can say, 'He loved me so much that he was prepared to die on the cross for me, to pay for my sins.' We have to ask the non-Christian, 'Who do you know who would be prepared to die for you?' To know Jesus, through his Spirit, and to know that he, the Son of God, loves us like that is a great source of strength, peace and security in life – which no one can take away.

So Christian faith not only promises us a wonderful future, it also gives us very practical ways of being upbeat about present life. That is the second reason it is worthwhile being a Christian. This is also the second reason why every community needs a good church to share Christ with them.

But there is a third reason why all communities need churches.

Because everybody needs a point to their lives (vv. 10-12).
This wonderful future prospect of life in God's new world, and the present experience of knowing Jesus by faith, Peter calls 'salvation' / 'rescue.' He has already mentioned the word in verse 5 and verse 9 and now he says (vv. 10-12), 'Concerning this salvation, the prophets, who spoke of the grace that was to come to you, searched diligently...It was revealed to them that they were not serving themselves but you, when they spoke of the things that have now been told you by those who preached the gospel to you by the Holy Spirit sent from heaven. Even angels long to look into these things.'

I was reading recently of a journalist who specialises in going to the most dangerous, war torn places in the world to bring the news. Someone asked him why he did it when it was so dangerous. His answer was that it was only when he was in such dicey situations that he felt really alive.

There are many people like that. Somehow, ordinary life leaves them feeling bored and un-special, so they court danger or go in for extreme sports or whatever. Human beings have a deep need to feel that their life is really significant, that they are special. But the consumer, information technology, TV couch potato society we live in makes us feel we are just a number on a card, just another member of the audience.

However, Peter is telling us here that to be a Christian is to be a very special person, someone who is the recipient of an amazing privilege. You are the object of God's plan of salvation.

The Bible is written in two parts, Old Testament and New Testament, with about 400 years between. The Old Testament prophets had something of God's plan of salvation, sending his Son, the Messiah, revealed to them. And they were astonished. 'What is this? Who are these people that God is so concerned for?' They were told hundreds of years in advance how the Messiah would suffer (the fulfilment of such prophecies like Isaiah 53 of course are yet another proof of the reality of God and of Christian faith) and of how the kingdom of God would spread through the earth (as we see today) and the glory that would follow, the new life, the living hope of the new world to come. 'Who is this focused on?' the prophets asked. Peter tells us (v. 12). It is us! It is people who are Christians. Peter was writing to first century Christians. We are twenty-first century

Christians. But we all enjoy the amazing privilege of salvation. That's why it is worthwhile to be a Christian. There are no more privileged people anywhere in the world!

And the people of every community in our land need the opportunity to hear about this privilege which is offered to them, which will redeem them from the pointless life of secular consumerism which ultimately leads to destruction.

God's mercy

But there is one last thing to notice. Look at verse 3. This is all of God's mercy. This salvation is not given because we deserve it or we have earned it by being better than other people. It is not merited through endless good deeds and religious rituals.

It is all about God's mercy. The story is told of a soldier in Napoleon's army who was court-martialled for an offence and sentenced to death. The soldier's mother, in deep distress, somehow got to see the emperor to plead for his life. 'Have mercy on my son,' she asked Napoleon. 'Why?' said the emperor, 'what has he done to deserve it?' She replied, 'Sir, if he deserved it then it wouldn't be mercy.'

This needs to be emphasized because there is an almost universal misunderstanding about salvation which has to be continually countered. If you ask most ordinary people about God and who goes to heaven when they die, they usually will reply in terms of heaven being for 'good' people and hell being for 'bad' people. They think that salvation is something which is earned by being good. Then, because all of us are self-deluded sinners, we all tend to see ourselves in the best light and to be able to convince ourselves as to why our bad

34

deeds were not really that bad. That means that the majority of people imagine that should they die, they will be acceptable to God. But, of course, this is a lie. If we could make ourselves acceptable to God there would have been no reason why Jesus should come and die for us. In reality, our goodness is a sham and to trust in our own goodness is to be lost (Rom. 3:20). And when local churches close, the tragedy is that a whole community of people is left believing this lie and there is no one to tell them otherwise.

The truth is that we are saved not by our own deserving, but by the mercy of God through Jesus Christ.

Every community needs to hear that there is forgiveness of sins and free salvation for all who trust in Jesus Christ. And that is why every local community needs a good church.

CHAPTER 4
HOW TO MAKE A SMALL
CHURCH A GREAT CHURCH

Small churches can become great churches. It can be done.

A close friend of mine was the prayer secretary in the Christian Union during university days. As Christians we shared a flat with others. He was (and is) an excellent zealous Christian and simply for reasons of being aware that he would not want attention drawn to himself, I will not give you his name.

In the mid-1970s he was called as a very young man to pastor a small church in a Midlands town. The situation was a classic of discouragement. The church building was a great barn of a place in a state of some dilapidation and the congregation had dwindled to perhaps twenty or a dozen mainly elderly folk. But, nevertheless my friend felt the call of God to take it on.

As a young preacher, I remember speaking there myself to help out on a number of occasions. With the congregation so small, they no longer met in the main worship area but in a little hall above the entrance to the building. This was kept warm by a couple of Calor gas heaters the fumes of which tended to have a soporific effect. It was quite a feat even to keep the ancient saints awake throughout an evening service.

What a situation! For many years nothing much seemed to happen, except a few minor encouragements from time to time. Though the preaching was good, the church continued fairly small. But my friend stuck to the task, praying, preaching and doing whatever he could, with the help of a faithful few, to make the little flock a group of Christians pleasing to Christ. And after something like fifteen years of his ministry there, suddenly the church took off. Christians moving into the area began to join, people began to get saved. Things they had only dreamed of before as a church began to come true. The church now numbers something like 200 to 250 people on Sundays, the building has been renovated and they have been used by God to plant another church in a nearby town.

Numbers are not everything. I believe this church had already become a great church even before the attendance began to increase. But the point is the church had been turned around. Instead of just surviving it is thriving. Such transformations do happen. With God's help, it can be done.

Therefore, despite the shower of cold water which I threw over you in chapter 2 let me once again encourage you to realize the potential of churches which are small.

So, we need to ask, should you decide to join such a small church what needs to be done? How can you help to make it the best it can be for Christ? What kind of strategy must be put into practice to bring out its full potential? How can we make a small church a great church?

Here are seven suggestions.

1. Be local

In our sceptical society non-Christians need not just to hear the message of God's love, but to see it lived out before their eyes. 'There are so many faiths and ideas around today,' unbelievers say, 'why should I believe you have the truth?' Sadly it is true that there are plenty of cults and religions which seek to turn people into mindless zombies and suicide bombers. Therefore we can sympathise somewhat with the non-Christian's sentiment.

If they don't know us very well why should they trust us? That is why just putting a tract through someone's door, or cold-calling and giving people who don't know you from Adam an invitation to church, is very unlikely to get anywhere in times like ours. But if we live in the area of the church people not only have the opportunity to know the church but also to know us personally. We have the opportunity to earn their trust. So to make a small church a great church, not only attend it, but go and live near it.

- Send your children to the local school
- Shop at the local shops
- Walk, don't drive. You don't meet anyone when you drive

2. Be involved

Be involved in the church, but also be involved in the community. This follows on from the last point. It is no good living in the area if we are going to shut ourselves away like some kind of religious recluse. Jesus loved people and so should we.

He showed his love for people in practical ways and so should we. He encourages us to 'Let your light shine before men, that they may see your good deeds and praise your Father in heaven,' Matthew 5:16. There is so much that can be done to help others in need, from young one-parent families who struggle with poverty to elderly people who can no longer do their own shopping and everything in between.

In the early centuries the church made great inroads through its kindness and service to the needy. In those days, anybody who did not believe in the Roman gods was called an 'atheist.' That included Christians! The Roman emperor Julian who tried to revive the old pagan worship was furious because of the love Christians showed. He wrote, 'Atheism has been especially advanced through the loving service rendered to strangers, and through their care and burial of the dead. It is a scandal that there is not a single Jew who is a beggar, and that the godless Galileans (Christians) care not only for their own poor but for ours as well...' It is this kind of loving service which will make any gospel church a great church – including a small one. Here are some things which churches do to get you thinking.

- Clean graffiti from the local subway
- Host a mothers and toddlers group for the community
- Run a support group for the recently divorced
- Open your premises for a club for the elderly or disabled free of charge

3. Be immoveable

A church needs stability. That only comes as key people stay. Thinking outside the church to the lost we are seeking to save, winning people's trust takes time. Therefore, not only move into the area and get involved in the church, but stick with it. The ethos of the consumer culture in which we live militates against this. It always encourages to be on the move, shopping around. David Wells writes about the US and tells us: 'In 2001, for example, while 8% switched to Catholicism, 17% switched out of it; 19% of those in Methodism were new but 25% left; 24% came into Presbyterianism but 25% disappeared; 30% were drawn into Pentecostalism but 19% departed. This, however, appears to be more of a cultural phenomenon than a purely Christian affliction because in this same year, 33% switched into Buddhism and 23% switched out.' (*Above All Earthly Pow'rs, IVP page 271*) To keep chopping and changing, switching churches etc., is the spirit of the age. Meanwhile perseverance and stick-ability is the way of the Spirit of God, Philippians 1:6.

- Still be there when the children who came to your children's club have children of their own
- Still be there when those who said they were too busy for church have now retired

4. Be faithful

There are many things which we can afford to change in a church. But the one thing which we cannot afford to change is the gospel we preach. We must preach the apostolic gospel as we find it in the New Testament. This gospel is 'the power of God for the salvation of everyone who believes,' Romans 1:16. It is this gospel which saves and no other, Galatians 1:8,9. Many Christians think that if we are going to make any impact for Christ then we need to gain public approval. So we are tempted to reshape and repackage the gospel in a way which is more immediately attractive to post-modern non-Christians. But that is the way to lose the gospel. The apostle Paul tells us that the minds and hearts of unbelievers are darkened. Their thinking, in spiritual terms, is futile, 2 Corinthians 4:4; Romans 1:21, 22.

To change the gospel to suit the world's foolishness will be to destroy it. The pressure is on to deny that sin is a real problem, or that there is such a thing as God's wrath, or that at the cross Jesus took the punishment for our sins, or that it is only those who trust in Jesus who are saved, or that only the Holy Spirit can really give people a new life. Such ideas don't go down very well in the present politically correct climate of the Western world. But they are the truth and we must be faithful. Great churches identify the real problem with people and lovingly hold out the great news of the gospel.

- Encourage the pastor to work through the church's doctrinal statement in the Sunday preaching from time to time

5. Be witnessing
We must not only know the truth, but of course, we must share it with others. This can be done in all kinds of ways as is appropriate to a church's situation.

But God will give those opportunities especially through our kindness and friendship towards others. One young woman was a single parent with four children by two different fathers. Her first marriage had ended in divorce and the second relationship had turned nasty. There was domestic violence before the man left. Battered and in need she shared her problems over the succeeding days with other parents in the school play ground. Some didn't want to know, but others rallied around to help as they could. It later dawned on her that in fact all the people who really showed care and tried to help her were Christians! Now, she wanted to know what this Christianity was all about. Now she was wide open to listen to the gospel and came through to trust in Christ. Kindness leads on to witness.

Another good Christian I know who is part of a small fellowship in the West Country was phoned up one evening by her hairdresser. 'Can I come and speak to you?' she asked. 'Why?' replied my friend, 'it is usually me asking for an appointment with you.' But the hairdresser explained that she wanted to come and ask her questions about Christian faith. Whenever my friend went to the shop, then within the usual chat that goes on between hairdresser and customer she did her best to mention her Christian experience or something about the church. Now, as the Spirit of God had been at work in the woman's heart that simple witness was bearing fruit. It was not long before the hairdresser came to Christ.

- Think through local situations which might give you natural opportunities for personal witness
- Put on regular evangelistic suppers at the church which will be relevant to ordinary people

- Have an annual scheme of delivering tracts or invitations to Christmas and Easter events around the local area

6. Be prayerful

Prayer works, Luke 11:13. It is no good simply complaining about the hardness of people's hearts and lamenting that so few are interested in the gospel. The little church which would see things change must give itself to prayer. Our society is very hard and only the power of God can break through. The small church must revive the prayer meeting and seek God.

Richard Bewes (who had a great ministry in recent years at All Souls, Langham Place in London) writes, 'The work of God cannot be undertaken without prevailing intercessory prayer. *Indeed we must go further and insist that prayer actually is the work.*' In other words, if we are not praying we are not working, so is it any surprise if nothing happens? Start praying yourself; wrestle in prayer and encourage others to do the same.

- Never miss the church prayer meeting
- Set up a few prayer groups for two or three people in the church, which meet at times convenient for them.

7. Believe God

It was a hot summer's day. I had the emergency exit door of a corridor in our church building open to get some air moving through the building in an attempt to keep cool. Suddenly as I was working away on my books a blackbird flew into my office. Flying against the window panes and realising that they did not present a way out it started to panic. I was worried it was going to hurt itself as it flew about the room and crashed against the glass. I don't know if it did any good, but I began to talk to it in a friendly and hopefully soothing way. It eventually calmed down and I was able to gently take it in my hands, take it outside and release it. It flew away chirping loudly.

Some small churches panic. They feel as if they are locked into a situation and there is no way out. At this point the few members can begin to turn on one another, blaming each other. Such situations require a cool head. It demands the wisdom of peacemaking. It calls for the wisdom of encouragement. It necessitates the wisdom of sound judgement. But in particular it requires faith. We must believe God. It is his church not ours. He cares about it even more than we do. We must believe that the expansion of his kingdom is always his will. We must believe that he wants us, as he wants all disciples to be useful to his purpose. We must put ourselves totally at God's disposal and take Jesus at his word that, 'Everything is possible for him who believes,' Mark 9:23. There is a way out. God is with us. We are his people. He will have a way.

- Encourage your faith by reading the biographies of great Christian men and women of the past whom God has used
- Read through the Bible with an eye to learning all you can about faith in God in the context of difficult situations

Notice the orientation of all these suggestions. They are directed outward from the church. Churches never become great by being self-pitying and ingrown. They become great as they nurture a genuine love for the glory of God and for the souls of lost men and women.

I recently watched a debate between a Christian apologist and an atheist professor. Having dismissed the resurrection of Jesus the atheist sneeringly remarked, 'Well anyway, what's this supposed God of yours been doing for the last 2000 years!' The answer, of course, is that he has been doing precisely what he said he would do, saving people from every tribe, tongue and nation. And, as yet another proof of God's reality, we see this happening all over the world today before our very eyes. Saving souls is what God is doing these days. Rescue is his end-time business before the Second Coming of Christ. So if we want God to use and bless our church, large or small, we had better be involved in that business.

CHAPTER 5
ENCOURAGEMENT FOR THE TASK

Oswald Smith was a Canadian pastor who lived from 1889 to 1986 and was famous for being the pastor who encouraged mission and missionaries.

The story is told that when he first arrived at what was to become The People's Church in Toronto, the congregation was small and was on the brink of closing down. But on his first Sunday in the pulpit he preached twice on world mission. Then, at the mid-week meeting, attended by just a few, he spoke again about world mission.

Eventually one of the elderly ladies plucked up courage to speak to him about this. Perhaps we can understand her sentiments. 'Mr. Smith,' she said, 'you are preaching about the need to take the gospel to the ends of the earth. But our church is on the verge of closing its doors because we are so few.' He replied, 'Sister, if we do not have enough conviction to desire to proclaim this message to the ends of the earth, our church will die.' With this conviction and vision the church grew enormously and became famous for its support of hundreds of missionaries all over the world.

Smith took on a small situation, but refused to be merely parochial. He was not prepared to let the outwardly meagre circumstances dictate his view of what could be achieved. Under God, this is the essence of Biblical faith. Faith sees the word of God and the promises of God as more real and reliable than all the apparent obstacles. It looks beyond the immediate conditions to the power of God to accomplish all he has planned. 'Now faith is being sure of what we hope for and certain of what we do not see' (Heb. 11:1).

Secular propaganda

We live in an age which tells us that only what is big is significant; only what attracts mass audiences is influential; only those who can deploy vast resources of cash or people are truly powerful. This is the obvious assumption which flows from an outlook of philosophical materialism which tells us that this world is all there is and only what we can see with our eyes has any reality. It is easy for us to fall into accepting this secular propaganda. When we do that we can end up writing off that which appears pint-sized and weak. We can end up hoping that whatever happens, and whatever he asks of us, God doesn't call us to a small church.

But, of course, the Bible teaches us a very different set of guidelines from that of the secular world. It teaches us that the unseen God is actually sovereign over all we see. It teaches us that prayer in Jesus' name works. It teaches us that 'nothing is impossible with God,' Luke 1:37. In getting involved with a small church we will need encouragement to grasp these truths and live by them. This can be a struggle. But we need to cultivate in ourselves the same kind of faith which motivated Oswald Smith.

Seven encouragements

If we take on helping a small church we will certainly face doubts and worries. We will be tempted, at least sometime or another, to think that we are wasting our time.

Here then, can I suggest seven encouragements which might help us to persevere and to believe that God can achieve great things through a small church.

1. The potential of the church is far greater than we realise
The Lord Jesus is the temple of God, the place where heaven meets earth and man meets God. But because Christians are joined to Christ by faith, Paul is able to speak of the local church as the house or temple of God, 1 Corinthians 3:16. As God's people struggled to rebuild the Old Testament temple, the Lord gave Zechariah the prophet an extraordinary vision to encourage the temple builders, Zechariah 1:18-22. He saw four great horns, symbols of strength and power. God explained that these represented the empires and worldly powers which had previously destroyed Jerusalem, scattering its people and taking them into exile. But then, the prophet was shown four craftsmen. 'What are these coming to do?' asked Zechariah. Listen to God's remarkable answer. 'The craftsmen have come to terrify them and throw down these horns of the nations

who lifted up their horns against the land.' In the context of rebuilding the temple, the craftsmen are those who are working on the house of God. God's temple (because it is the house where God dwells) is able to overthrow the nations! Translating this into New Testament terms, just so, we must believe that God's church (because Christ himself dwells among us, Matthew 28:20) has the potential to overthrow all worldly opposition and be victorious for the kingdom of God.

2. The Lord is able to use small groups of Christians to transform whole communities.

This should not surprise us. Often Paul's missionary band consisted of just a few people. But such was the impact of such Christian outreach that they were accused of 'turning the world upside down.'

When US troops captured the Pacific island of Okinawa towards the end of WWII they found it in a state of moral and social collapse. But as they gradually advanced through the island, they came to the village of Shimbakuku. There they were greeted by two men – one carrying a Bible.

The soldiers entered the village cautiously, but were amazed to find everything neat and tidy, in contrast to the almost total chaos elsewhere. Why? 30 years earlier a missionary had stopped in Shimbakuku on his way to Japan. He didn't stay long and just two people, the old men, had become Christians. He left a Bible, urging them to shape their lives by it. Following the Bible alone, others became Christians and the whole community was transformed. So the soldiers found no jail, no brothel, no drunkenness – just humble, contented people.

The war correspondent who first brought this story to light was Clarence Hall. He quoted his dumbfounded driver, who said, 'So this is what comes out of only a Bible and a couple of old men who want to live like Jesus! Maybe we're using the wrong kind of weapons to change the world.' They transformed the community; a Bible and a couple of old men. Does that sound like a small church to you? It does to me!

3. The Lord is able to use the most unlikely people to do remarkable things

Some years ago now, I found that I had a namesake, John Benton, who was used by God during the times of the Methodist revival in and around the Potteries area of Stoke-on-Trent and Staffordshire. His story took me aback when I read it.

This John Benton was an uneducated man who was not at all naturally gifted as a speaker. He had little or no sense of grammar or good English. Converted to Christ and full of zeal for the Lord he often tried to share the gospel with others. But such was his roughness of speech and lack of education that he was forbidden to speak by the local vicar. However, one day John Benton found himself preaching to a group of miners beside the road. The Spirit of God came upon the gathering and the men were under conviction of sin, possibly with tears flowing. Just at that moment, the vicar who had forbidden him to preach came around the corner and saw the sight. John Benton turned to him, pointed him to these men on whom God was evidently at work, and said to the vicar, 'Look, there's my grammar!' The lesson is obvious. If God can use a man like John Benton he can use any of us!

4. The Lord Jesus said he will build his church

The Lord Jesus, the carpenter of Nazareth, said: 'I will build my church, and the gates of hell will not prove stronger than it' (Matt. 16:18).

We are here told that the building of Jesus' church takes place against the background of fierce opposition. We are warned in advance therefore that there will be difficulties. In a sense, the fact that the churches are up against it in our day is normal. But Christ has promised that all the opposition which the devil himself can throw at the church will not prevail. Therefore we are to have great faith as we seek to help a small church. The fact of Christ's power for his church has been marvellously demonstrated for us in recent years. During most of the twentieth century Christians under Communism faced ferocious persecution. Sometimes during those dreadful years we must have wondered how the church in those countries could survive. But in 1989 Communism in Eastern Europe collapsed. After all that persecution it was not the church which folded, but Communism itself. The gates of hell shall not prevail. Christ is stronger. Therefore, believe he can build his church.

5. The Lord's power is not dependent on great human resources

The governor of the Jews during the time that they were seeking to rebuild the temple was Zerubbabel. He was born in Babylon (that's what his name means) and now returning from the exile he was the civic leader, responsible to the Persian emperor.

In Judah it was a day of small things. The Jews had returned to a devastated land, much diminished in size. The harvests had not been good and everyone felt poor and had decided that now was obviously not the right time to rebuild God's temple. But God's encouraging word came through Zechariah the prophet to Zerubbabel. 'This is the word of the Lord to Zerubbabel: Not by might nor by power, but by my Spirit, says the LORD Almighty' (Zech. 4:6). The word 'might' here is used in the Old Testament of armies of soldiers or armies of workers such as Solomon had to build the original temple (1 Kings 5:13-18). It refers to collective strength, to what you can do with big numbers of people. But God specifically says that he does not need large numbers. That is an encouragement for a small church. The word 'power' is about individual ability. Surely the key to making God's work successful is an individual of great brilliance, or of commanding character and enormous energy. 'That's what we need – someone who is an international athlete, or from a celebrity family, with a few degrees and letters after his name.' But God says he does not need this either. That is a great encouragement to a church of ordinary people. God is able to do all he desires through the power of his Spirit.

6. The power of God's Spirit is available to all Christians
Sometimes we think that it is only in big groups of people that the Lord can do great things by his Spirit. But that is not true. Jesus said that where even two or three gather in his name he is there among them. Further, his presence was not limited to the first century. He told us plainly that he would be with us until the very end of the world, Matthew 28:20.

The Lord, as we know, has been doing astonishing things in China in the last 20 to 30 years, with millions of people being saved. Not long ago one of the British broadsheet newspapers reported that there are now more Christians in China than card-carrying Communists!

It is interesting to read the agreed statement of faith put out by the Chinese house churches in 1998. 'In Christ God grants a diversity of gifts of the Holy Spirit to the church so as to manifest the glory of Christ. Through faith and thirsting, Christians can experience the outpouring and filling of the Holy Spirit.' It was that word 'thirsting' which struck me. Do we thirst for the Spirit and the glory of God? Surely there is a case for saying that people in small churches are less likely to be happy with the *status quo* and therefore more open to thirst for the Spirit of God's work. How to get ourselves thirsting? Think of what might be if God moves by his Spirit. Think of the conversions. Think of the joy in families, the lives changed! Think of the love and genuine kindness in the church! Think of the local community renewed as they come to know Christ! Do this and we begin to thirst.

But Jesus said, 'If anyone is thirsty let him come to me and drink,' John 7:38. It is the Lord Jesus who pours out his Spirit and tells us that anyone is free to come and drink. That includes us.

7. The breakdown of secular society is a sign of how much each community needs a church

The beginning of the twenty-first century in Britain has been sadly notable for a marked decline in the quality of life and civilized conduct. Not only has family breakdown become common but the culture of drugs and its attendant crime, together with binge drinking and thuggish behaviour have become prevalent. A recent survey published in *Time* magazine reported that one fifth of Britons do not go out at night rather than risk becoming a target for violent groups of young people on the streets.

We should not be surprised at this. The Bible tells us that where a nation rejects God, all kinds of wicked behaviour results. But, however we view this breakdown of society which we are experiencing, it is a clear sign to us that the gospel and therefore our churches, big or small, are needed.

Therefore, we are not to believe the doubts and fears that the little church is irrelevant or that we are wasting our time in giving our energies to its life and outreach. Rather, we are, in faith, to look beyond our circumstances to the sure promises of God, and work hard for him. And in the light of eternity we shall find that we have spent our lives in the best possible way.

Therefore, my dear brothers, stand firm. Let nothing move you. Always give yourselves fully to the work of the Lord, because you know that your labour in the Lord is not in vain.

1 Corinthians 15:58

EPILOGUE
AN IRRECOVERABLE MOMENT?

I disagree with Henry Ford who famously declared, 'History is bunk!' Actually many historical events are not only great sources of inspiration, but also contain vital lessons for today. And there is a great lesson to be learned about the usefulness of what is small from one particular operation during the Second World War.

By the early summer of 1940 the Nazi armies had broken the French and Belgian defences and the British Expeditionary Force was in full retreat. Hundreds of thousands of troops were stranded in the town and on the beaches of Dunkirk on the French side of the Channel at the mercy of the Luftwaffe and the German Panzers. An evacuation plan codenamed 'Operation Dynamo' was hastily put into action to ferry the beleaguered British, French and Belgian soldiers back to England.

It was expected that perhaps 30,000 troops could be saved. But, in the event, from late May through into June, under constant attack from the air, the ships were able to save no less than 338,000 allied soldiers to fight another day. Winston Churchill, the British Prime Minister, called it a 'miracle of deliverance.'

But how did it happen? What was the key to this great escape? Crucial to the success of this rescue operation were the 'little ships' – the motor yachts, fishing smacks, dinghies, pleasure craft and paddle steamers which got involved in this very dangerous operation. They were crucial, because once Dunkirk harbour became blocked with sunken vessels, the troops had to be taken off the beaches, which the large ships could not get near. But what the big boats could not do, the 'little ships' could.

Little ships / small churches
Just so, the church today is involved in a great rescue operation, seeking to save the souls of men and women. And just as at Dunkirk, it would seem that the 'little ships' (small churches) have a crucial role to play. The large churches of our land tend to be in the cities and big towns, often miles away from the areas where many ordinary people live. To go there to church is a half hour's car ride if not more. But there are still small churches which are local, and can get right alongside those in need of salvation. They are just around the corner. They operate right there where the people live, not miles away. This is why small churches are crucial. This is why it is worth joining a church local to where you live.

And God is using small churches today.

Another real-life story which comes to mind is of a little

fellowship tucked away in the backwaters of a quiet village in East Anglia. Its building is a typical old 'tin tabernacle' which would not win many design awards for architecture today. However, through the people of the church making themselves useful to the village, through things like a mothers-and-toddlers group, the church has begun to grow. People are coming in. People are getting saved. As I write, the church has had to think through how it can expand the building to cope with the newcomers; and the Lord is providing the finance. God uses small churches. Never doubt it.

Opportunity, but for how long?

In his autobiography, *Just As I Am,* the famous evangelist Billy Graham tells of a missed opportunity.

Just after his election, Billy Graham had a conversation with President John F. Kennedy. The President had asked if the evangelist really believed in the Second Coming of the Lord Jesus Christ. Billy Graham told him he did and explained one or two things about it. 'Very interesting,' Kennedy had said, 'We'll have to talk more about that someday.' Then they parted.

A few years later, Graham and Kennedy's paths crossed again, at the 1963 National Prayer Breakfast. 'I had flu,' Billy Graham recalls. 'After I gave my short talk and he gave his, we walked out of the hotel to his car together...At the curb, he turned to me. "Billy, could you ride back to the White House with me? I'd like to see you for a minute." "Mr. President, I've got fever," I protested. "Not only am I weak, but I don't want to give you this thing. Couldn't we wait and talk some other time?"

'It was a cold, snowy day, and I was freezing as I stood there without my overcoat. "Of course", he said graciously.'

But the two never met again. Later that year John F. Kennedy was shot dead.

Billy Graham comments, 'His hesitation at the car door, and his request, haunt me still. What was on his mind? It was an irrecoverable moment.'

Reading this we feel for Billy Graham. He had missed an opportunity which never came again.

As we conclude this little booklet encouraging Christians to get involved with small churches, I feel I must press the invitation by reminding you that it may well be that this present time is 'an irrecoverable moment' for the church in our land.

If Christians do not take up the challenge to join small churches and get involved with these works soon, then within a generation the vast majority of them will be gone. If younger Christians are only interested in big, 'successful', 'all-singing all-dancing' churches, then the small churches all over our land will close. The light of the gospel will go out in countless communities. And it seems more than likely that those gospel lights will never be lit again.

Make or break?

Many young people have been drawn into an 'entertainment' view of Sunday worship by what I will call 'big church culture.' They are attracted to the services by the 'performances' of a spectacular music group or a big name preacher with his superbly crafted sermon. Such things are simply not to be had in the majority of small churches. Sadly, even unwittingly, many large churches are thereby fostering a culture which, as it stands, probably guarantees the demise of small churches. Will the large churches be prepared to change this? The rising generation of young Christians are often groomed (unintentionally?) to become religious consumers who treat churches like spiritual supermarkets, not to become humble servants willing to take on uncomfortable situations for the wider needs of Christ's kingdom. But if small churches close, our land will be even more spiritually impoverished than it already is. The next ten to twenty years will be the make or break.

To join a small church and be useful to God is the opportunity of a lifetime. But unless Christians take up the challenge within less than a lifetime that opportunity will be gone.

Why not join a small church?

The Transforming Community:
The Practise of the Gospel in Church Discipline
Mark Lauterbach

Jesus, in his ministry, received the empty, the broken, the lost and the diseased. Mark Lauterbach shows how compassion, mediated through a functioning body of believers, provides the answers to human waywardness and maintains the integrity of the church.

Although this is a book about church discipline, it is really about a spirit-empowered community. Mark uses real situations from his experience to help us turn principles into practice.

'...a biblically sensitive and pastorally wise book on a subject many people would just as soon forget about: accountability among Christians. True church discipline is not about reinforcing legalisms but rather nurturing believers with a covenanted community of faith.'

Timothy George, Dean,
Beeson Divinity School of Samford University

'I have never read a book like this or even close to this. Written with a rare combination of biblical insight, and seasoned compassion, born of many years "in the trenches" of local church leadership.'

Dr. Ray Pritchard, Senior Pastor,
Calvary Memorial Church, Illinois

ISBN 978 1 85792 875 4

Preparing Your Church for Revival
T M Moore

We all long for revival, but we tend to pray for it to come without being completely sure what precisely revival is. This book will be a revitalising aid to those of us who desire revived spiritual life for our churches. T. M. Moore offer practical advice on steps, each with secure scriptural foundations, that we can take to prepare our churches for the sovereign work that is revival. This book is clear that there is no conflict between revival being a work of God and the continued and urgent need for God's people to earnestly pray for its appearance. With practical guides to prayer for revival T. M. Moore realises the need for balance and succeeds in providing a book that will help us to refocus on revival, and will prepare our souls and our churches for the mighty work of a Sovereign and loving God.

T. M. Moore is a Fellow with the Wilberforce Forum and Pastor of Teaching Ministries at Cedar Springs Presbyterian Church in Knoxville, Tennessee. His essays, reviews, articles and poetry have appeared in a wide range of journals, and he is the author of more than ten books.

ISBN 978 1 85792 698 9

Christian Focus Publications
publishes books for all ages

Our mission statement –

STAYING FAITHFUL

In dependence upon God we seek to help make His infallible Word, the Bible, relevant. Our aim is to ensure that the Lord Jesus Christ is presented as the only hope to obtain forgiveness of sin, live a useful life and look forward to heaven with Him.

REACHING OUT

Christ's last command requires us to reach out to our world with His gospel. We seek to help fulfil that by publishing books that point people towards Jesus and help them develop a Christ-like maturity. We aim to equip all levels of readers for life, work, ministry and mission.

Books in our adult range are published in three imprints.

Christian Focus contains popular works including biographies, commentaries, basic doctrine and Christian living. Our children's books are also published in this imprint.

Mentor focuses on books written at a level suitable for Bible College and seminary students, pastors, and other serious readers. The imprint includes commentaries, doctrinal studies, examination of current issues and church history.

Christian Heritage contains classic writings from the past.

Christian Focus Publications, Ltd
Geanies House, Fearn, Ross-shire,
IV20 1TW, Scotland, United Kingdom
info@christianfocus.com
www.christianfocus.com